Bones & Breath

ALEXANDER HUTCHISON brought out *Scales Dog: Poems New and Selected* from Salt in 2007, and earlier books include *The Moon-Calf* and *Carbon Atom*. His first collection, *Deep-Tap Tree* – which Richard Ellmann said was 'compounded of wit and mystery' – remains in print. Born in Buckie, Hutchison now lives in Glasgow, has taken to singing a bit more, and still likes to turn up for a kickabout on a red ash pitch on Sundays.

Bones & Breath

ALEXANDER HUTCHISON

SALT

CROMER

PUBLISHED BY SALT PUBLISHING
12 Norwich Road, Cromer, Norfolk NR27 0AX

© Alexander Hutchison, 2013

The right of Alexander Hutchison to be identified as the
author of this work has been asserted by him in accordance
with Section 77 of the Copyright, Designs and Patents Act 1988.

Salt Publishing 2013

Printed in the UK by Berforts Information Press Limited

Typeset in Paperback 9 / 13

ISBN 978 1 907773 61 7 hardback

1 3 5 7 9 8 6 4 2

Contents

1	1
Bones & Breath	3
Adrift Is Maybe Not the Word	4
Chopping Down the Beanstalk	5
True as Tides	6
Aye, Plenty, an Mair	7
Gavia Stellata	8
Parable of the Willow	10
Tabouleh	12
Tin Cup	14
2	15
Camp Four	17
Wappenschaw	24
3	25
Out of Magma, the Moon: a Witness	27
Hermeneutics	30
The Daftie Names His Tunes	31
Deil Tak the Hinmaist	32
Matter and Moisture	34
24 and 26 to Be Precise	44
The Welcome	45
Tod	46
Everything	48
4	51
Setting the Time Aside	53
5	65
Tardigrade	67
Notes	79

Acknowledgements

Thanks to the editors of the following, where some of these poems previously appeared: *Birdbook 2* (Sidekick Books); *Gutter*; *Painted, spoken*; *Scottish Review of Books*; *The Dark Horse*; *The International Literary Quarterly*, http://interlitq. org; *The Long Poem Magazine*; *The Poem*; *The Syllabary*; www. thesyllabary.com

'Setting the Time Aside' was included in Andrew Greig's choice of *Best Scottish Poetry 2009*, http://www.spl.org.uk/ poetry/best-scottish-poems/best-scottish-poems-2009

'Aye, Plenty, an Mair' won a McCash Prize in 2009.

Several pieces were first printed in *Alexander Hutchison: Poeta di Scozia* (*In Forma di Parole* 4th series 3, Bologna 2010) with translations into Italian by Alessandro Valensizi.

'Deil Tak the Hinmaist' appeared in Roddy Lumsden's selection of *The Best of British Poetry 2011* from Salt.

The poem *Tardigrade* was published as a pamphlet by Perjink Press, 2013.

Glad thanks to friends and family for help at every stage.

'And now good morrow to our waking soules,
Which watch not one another out of feare.'

1

Bones & Breath

Here's me
barely out
of the nest,
my mouth

rinsed: shadow
and shape
astir on dusty
ground.

Heart brims
and spills.

Words try
eyes and wings;
try *air*.

The bones light,
my breath light.

Adrift Is Maybe Not the Word

We were all attempting to avoid
damp patches, spent matches, old
snatches that couldn't raise a smile.
We were all vainly scraping around
for scant reward. No sap, no savour.
Song and 'puff' was all we had to
go on now. Plum duff or porridge
in a drawer would not sustain us.

We were all hoping for something
better, to put it frankly; something
we could all get stuck properly into:
mulch and compost, deep-cut ditches.
Fibrillators, respirators maybe not.
Flint-glance or twirling to conjure a
spark. Zygotes and teeny brain cells
brought extravagantly into play.

We were all maybe looking for
something that wasn't there, or
couldn't be touched, didn't exist.
Brisk, complex – or *un*complicated,
who's to say? Who's to hear?
Rope on, lighten up. Feel that? It's
whoa on the one hand, *whoa, whoa*;
on the other restive, omnivorous.

Chopping Down the Beanstalk

Clarions and fifes are filled, are
sounded, and though we cannot
take the atmosphere to pieces,
a little judicious levity will not go amiss.

Fie on cheats and foul deception;
negative fie for sheer delight. A kiss
is not a contract always. Cherish *lovely,
lazy things*. Whispers that wound may
yet fill wide-eyed wonder.

'Fine, Fife, fossil fishes those!' sits
well on a postcard. Fetch in the master
of the traverse flute. Shape and fit
our embouchure. Muskets and drums
should not go short of a partner.

Redemption is tempting, as oblivion
yawns. And not much happens with
fee . . . fo, fum if *fie* falls clean away.

True as Tides

'True as tides' the saying
goes in Newfoundland;
and 'sure as shit shoots
off a shovel' no doubt
that would go down too.

As to the name, the
middle syllable goes
unstressed by those
who live there. Slide

over the first two;
let your tongue come
down on 'land'. John
Donne was the boy
first traced its outline

mapped on his lady's
sine qua non. Though
'Look what I've found!'
didn't quite match his
quaint discovery, like
planting his standard
where *nothing else is.*

Aye, Plenty, an Mair

A'm nae aa that sure aboot Glumsh or Glunsh –
bit Grizzel an Happit are in aboord onywye.
Is the back door snibbit? Mak sure it's wide open.
There micht be some neebors cam throwe the back
gairden or in ower the waa. Golach and Glit were nivver
my bosom freens, bit ye winna keep them oot if there's
ither fowk in. A'm nae haein Drittle nor Fouter, though –
nane o them – there's aye some scutter or sotter wi yon.
Hud back the fancies – bit pit them oot later. Shortbreid
an tablet, an twa or three panjotteries – there wis nae
oofum-ploofums at the baker's the day. Bit there's broon
breid and pan loaf an butter an honey, an plinty o sassidges,
fae Tommy, the best. Ye can aye pit on tatties, there's broth
on the simmer, an fish winna keep. Oh, there's galshach
o some kind – jist mindit this meenit – in the press
oot the back. So rowe up the cairpets, redd the fleer,
space for dancin. Bring aabody ben as seen as they're in.
An mind noo fit I tell't ye: the finest particles are langest
suspendit, so maist o oor relatives are still t' come doon.

Gavia Stellata

Who calls to the dark?
Who, when the shadows
are converted to morning,
when light pours out, when
day is turned to darkness
once more, when dark
is on the face of the sea,
who dives down, who
brings back a speck
to build on? I do. I did.

Who is the smallest
and brightest
and speckled
with stars? I am.

All things that gather
to shine I bear on my back
I raise on my wings
in the black of the waters,
in the deep vault of space.

Who dips and dives?
Dense bones take me down.

Who rose with a twin,
with another, who breasted
the face of the night, who
stitched the belt of stars
in Orion? Who speeds

without drag: bill like an awl
and flattened tarsus, neatest
and fleetest in streamlined
propulsion? Who took
Arcturus like a morsel of light,
a pinch of snuff, returned
to the surface?

Who calls to the dark,
who calls to the wind on
the surface of the water?
Who prompts the others
to dip and rise? Eyes like
seeds of garnet. Lightest
and brightest: *gavia stellata*
the red-throated diver.

Parable of the Willow

Too much snow toppled
me last winter: two thirds
(more like *four-fifths*) of my
root system torn and tipped
out of the ground. Someone
should have shaken my top
branches or taken the weight
off elsewhere: all those trailing
yellow-green, tufted withies.

Now, though, I just continue
otherwise: kneeling forward,
propped on an elbow of grounded
upper trunk, dispatching here
and there some surreptitious
rooting saps that procreate in
points of good connection; getting
by on less than half and half again
of what stood straight and fully
fixed the year before.

Wry smile after deep groan
is more my style than weeping.
Finger touches gripping tight
to stay me up, and taking just
enough to keep me going. After
all, I'm not a carpenter's delight;
and not much good as wood
for the fire – I sputter and spark.
Measly heat with mounds of ash.

But cut and woven out of coppice,
wicker shelters, baskets, lobster pots
and plaited fences spurn the worm.
While cricket bat blades (the handle's
cane) may smack or waft the ball away.

From root to osier-tip, utility.

Reduced to fine, smooth charcoal
I can fix your life in bright and dark
of *chiaroscuro*. Salicylic acid soothes.
My bark applied or boiled as juice
will ease a stound, assuage an ache
in ligament or joint. That's solace
interlaced with healing. Wrap me
round your head for grief: from
severance you'll make a start.

A spare green tenacity keeps me here.
Latch on to that at least from what
I say, and turn it to some use before
a gusting wind or wanton weight
of weather bowls you over too,
and bows you down just so.

Tabouleh

Snapped open; snapped shut: I told you they would all turn
up sooner or later. At least one blur at the back, maybe two,
though pleasant enough. These canapés are disgusting;
and why would anyone want to touch the tabouleh? Over
there, our rubicund bargeman, aye, with the burgermeister's
pantry maid in frills and mascara. Move round a bit. Who let
them in? The guru and the Gorgon side by side, no doubt cooking
up another *croque* for brunch. Not as many as last year. What do
you think? There's Molly the Maori – and the Duchess just over,
waggling her rings, trying to explain away events of the previous
evening, though no one within fifteen metres believes her. Okay,
pass me one of those. Is that not *la veuve souriante* astraddle her
chair? She must have exhausted the money. Everything but
the picture frames and the fleet of vintage cars. Oh, and that's
a crisp personality sitting right up against the wall – the one
embroidered with lichen and periwinkles. Who said that? That's
quite good: the Mink and the Leveret. Always a compromise
between conflicting appetites. Look out – *behind you* – it's Jake
with his hair slicked back and the green furred teeth. Do you
remember that night in the old open air pool? It's rusted away
by now I wouldn't be surprised. As to that one I'm not quite
sure, but she used to go out with the owner of the Cracked
Crab Bistro. No, cracked crab. Oh, oh, it's the man from Pravda
or the sinister sub-minister of Eastern Approaches: bomb-sights
on Stettin or the Straits of Hormuz. I always liked those gold-
tipped cigarettes. Don't look now but there's the Bum Deal.

Am I right? No, that's him for sure. And that will be the messenger from Slèat with badly-built Bertha. There's Olly (and Ivy – ha, ha that's not funny); and the lassie with the yellow hair I promised to meet last Tuesday. A few still straggling in. Don't know any of that lot. But, look: Lady Drypoint straight in to gush or dissuade. Where's her usual tumescent partner? Had enough? That man, tweed waistcoat, looks like he could argue the price of a bullock. And, whoops, a fisherman with hooks in his looks and not in his hat. That's it for me. Perhaps one more glass; and a word – we *must* – with the three ugly sisters, or the prickly acerbic one at the door peering out into the ginger gloaming.

Tin Cup

You will come across
some strange versions
of organ-grinder
and monkey in any
line of work or art
or business enterprise;
it's true. And oft-times
it's hard to say precisely
who's grinding, who's
dancing, who's smiling
who's wagging
the little tin cup.

2

Camp Four

Well, here we are
again at Camp Four.
Will we press on to
the summit? 'As like
as not, with all that
gear and meagre talent.'

(A low, unwelcome
voice from a neighbouring
lair cuts through in the
most unhelpful fashion.)

Weather for the next
few days will shut
us down in any case;
the wind alone would
guarantee we make
no move at all.

*Harriet's leg may have
to come off, and not,
maybe* not, *before time.
I don't actually mind
the way it looks now;
but she maintains
it's gone quite
beyond a joke.*

2

The lentils are *kaput*
I'd warrant, leaving
what? Sauerkraut
chutney, desiccated beef.

So where do we go
from here? Sideways
or down? And who or what
do we hale to our assistance?

D-branes? *p-*
branes? Strings and loops;
inflationary bursts?

Gravitational waves
were from the first
unlikely to do the trick.

An increase in coupling,
constant or otherwise,
was never on the cards.

If I had known there
were going to be five
more camps beyond
this, I would have
taken longer, deeper
counsel than I did.

And, *alright*, another
starting point entirely.

3

These intervals make
little sense to me.
Even a 'fundamental
fabric' surely can be rent?

It's all very well
to dress up things
for children: dark matter
dark energy, with
little chirping spirits
plausible and catchy.

But get to an overhang
like this, and what is
there left to say?

We need joists to hoist
and meta-boats to lay
a keel for. Block and
Tackle have gone
to bed, believe me.

To compare is not to compose.

4

What can I add?

The exchange of light,
the ligatures of sound at
Camp Four, while greatly
improved, are not auspicious.

As it gathers to a head
how do we shake
off impediments?

*It won't be easy
to stifle a memory like
this: to trace outwith
the usual liminal bits
or frozen path fit
and fair resting
place for Harriet's
jettisoned limb.*

As for hydrogen
or carbon again, I
wouldn't hold your breath.

5

Companionship's not all
it's cracked up to be.
Though blows delivered
to the soles of the feet
with mercury rods
and, yes, *some subtlety*,
might help me stir.

Maybe we can vamp or
cobble together tomorrow,
ravel up those gaps.

Temporise and stuff
the holes with burlap.

*Sometimes it rotates,
or so they would
have us believe.*

I'll eat whatever's left.

6

No doubt you're ahead
of me, but with the future
fixed or translucent
at best, have we the means,
the truth, to measure it?

Keep an eye on the glass:
barometric pressure may
still tell us something.

(Though not which
habits or surfaces are
likely to give way.)

Perhaps some fresh
breath or turn, some
small shaped note of
sacrifice is due.

Filaments, connection
energy might still
be in the frame.

Dust won't do it.
Not this time.

7

When do we choose
who leads, and how?

Another length of rope
should not go amiss.

The final fly-leaf entry,
scrutinised again,
might offer a clue:

*'What will it take for
song and sense to make
all rise and flourish:
intensive, whole, aspiring?'*

Or follow that note
on a holograph slip –

*'Like out of a bell or
golden hive a stream
of bees in a luminous
swarm: reverberant
resounding.'*

I'm fairly sure, *convinced*
we can't ignore any of that,
unless sheer folly would
prove our guide.

Wappenschaw

'What's a wappenschaw?'

Well, this is a wappen.
And *this* is a schaw.

3

Out of Magma, the Moon: a Witness

Early that evening
as soon as I stepped
out, I saw a little
patch of peach and rose-
coloured light spilling
on the snow of the mountain's
sloping ridge. I had
my coat and scarf, but
not the new *coppola*
bought next day
in the *fiera all'aperto*
of nearby Randazzo.

Bareheaded in the chill
I leaned back in
along the wall and let
the wind blow by.
Though the mountain any
time is still composed
of ruinous fire, this
was no vented flame.
It was the moon.

It was the moon: not
reflecting from a cloud
but gradually rising
slowly like something
flowing from a forge
in a nimbus of silvery
rouge: something made

new like skin and flesh –
mis-shapen, yellowish
pale *mandarino* –
echo of fruit and fire.

Within three minutes
or four or so it had
assumed more usual
form (rounded, white
blue-silver) this
night beyond the full.
No one else to see
to tell, to point, to say.

But the white quick cat
with ginger-spotted coat
stepped out from a hedge
quick, quick, quick
across the cooling crust.

Snakes, abductions, golden
days and *suino nero*
make our stories rise
and flow, give bite
to life. But listen.
Each night the moon
charged with pale blood
rises from a fumarole
on Etna's fiery flank –

out of the earth's deep
fissured core, I swear –
there *'from out the dark*
door of the secret earth.'
And the wound is
healed straightaway.

Secure that cat
and it will tell you.
Just as I have
told you now.

Hermeneutics

Nae muckle caa noo for whins
and wheeps t' sort oot the elders.
Or linin up t' get a lick aff Mrs Lot.

Ye can aye get doon on yer hauns
an knees an lap wi yer tongue
if ye'r speirt t' tak watter.

Nae muckle else – unless
ye coont the barley breid
baps that flattened
the tents o Midian.

The Daftie Names His Tunes

from Villon

I ken flees in milk
I ken the jaikit mannie

I ken salad days
for the hamely quine

I ken the aipple
t' the aipple tree

I ken
aathin the same

I ken faa's yoakit
an faa's slack

I ken fit quidna
be pit oot

I ken aabody
exceptin masel.

Deil Tak the Hinmaist

'I think ye ocht t' pit the pillywinkies on t' him.'

The girt yett kickit in, an lo! – they liggit: *scummers o pots
an skelpers o cuddies*; jaws that cleikit, rhymes that reikit; Kerr's Pink
tatties biled in their jaickets; deedle-dabblers in cytoplasm; virtual
realtors swickin an swyvin; daddy-lang-legs; dirlin Dodies;
hoodie-craws cracklin fae the tippy-taps o trees:

> Deid-loss or Daidalos
> fit's it gaan tae be?

Pooshin pumpers, coonter-jumpers, cairpet fitters birslin wi a moo-fae
o tacks; tomcats, corncrakes; shilly-shally sharn shifters; couthy bicuspids;
aa the wee glisterin anes; aa them that wid grudge ye one jow o the bell.

The neist yett swung, syne mair wis kythit: tethered tups,
draigelt yowes; the slalom loons fae Dandruff Canyon; wheepers
o candy-floss; footerin futtrets; the hee-haw-hookum o hystet hizzies;
foosty fowk lik Finnan haddies; Buckie blaavers wi the full wecht o blaw.

Shouther tae the third yett, an jist as ye micht expeck: sornars
an sooks; herriers an haverers; gran chiels in blue corduroy, fantoosh
wifies; r.p. flannel dinkers; parkins, merkins; secont-sichtit seannachies
wi hunkies clappit t' their snoots; flunkeys, junkies; buglers, shooglers;
Methuselahs wi nips an tucks; trashtrie shotten aff the shelf.

> As douce a set o creepy-crawlies
> as ye're ivver like t' see.

Here-am-ur; hempseed; fushionless tail-toddle:
Daith's on the fussle lik the win throw the widdy.

Roon the corner, an doon the stair: polyglot thrapple-stappers;
chirpy chairmers; mingers an moochers; bracken for brakfast, neebors
for lunch. Lest bit nae least: flees in putty, wersh wicks in seas o wax.

Coda: Scoor it if ye fancy intil ae muckle plum duff –
plooms, suet, orange peel – simmert slaw an slaistert
in slices, faa's t' say it winna lest for years?

Matter and Moisture

1

Unlucky in the locations;
maybe in the weather too.

'What we pursue is matter
and moisture; what satisfies
or implicates us thoroughly
however is mostly wispy
nonsense to describe.'

He got to the point where
his heart just couldn't take
another butter biscuit; nor
his cortex another insult like
the one dished up before.

'Circle back or head on
anyway; anyhow you are
free to go. Thunder and rain,
the voice of pardon. Cracking
on and cracking open.'

Rumour, misunderstanding:
it's easy to take offence.

Outside, not a breath
of wind; but the birds
on the go very early.

Forgiveness brings release.

3

Just because something is
going round is no good reason
for you to catch it.

Have a cup of tea and put your
own dishes in the sink. Give them
a quick rinse then get some music on.
Don't bother with anyone else's.

That piece for clarinet is perfectly
consoling, but don't be tempted
to wallow. Judge for yourself.

If fingers wag, let them.

4

Scattered like stars on the ground
what we share is not an accident.

Even when we like the same things
doesn't make an alliance between us.

'Love binds; fear bonds.
Many pretend and dissimulate.'

If a little bit of light shows round
the edge of the door, that's okay.

You might have the sense of something
or somebody coming close to look over
your shoulder. You'll hear it when it comes.
Otherwise there's no need to stir.

5

I'll bring the scraper,
you bring the trowel and struts.

It's got to be cleared out properly.
Might as well be this afternoon.

We should start in front of the town
if not right opposite the gate.

It will take some time to get inside.

6

'Force of cunning in
the face of strength':

out of that dark
coil – something.

Better to come
half-way: I would.

Bickering is not
the best – even if
you are bound to.

'Ca canny: a good start
brings an end quicker.'

How often have we
had to listen to that?

But watch your tail in
the water, and watch what
you do with your feet.

7

'I wish I was really brave.
Perhaps I have changed now,
but I doubt it. I wish I had
something beyond hesitation:
heedless, unwavering.'

'Maybe I'm not as bad as once
I was. Children change things.
But it demeans me: all the rest
of virtue falls away without it.'

Confidence in doing things
willingness to take a risk or two,
to speak one's mind, or being
prepared to take the blame,
is not the same as being
prepared to take a blow.

8

Jackets off, tops too.
What's to stop us?

Going at it ding dong.
Fire and water.

Save your claws
and teeth right now,
but I don't doubt
you'll need them.

There's a metal post
with a pointed end, if
you want to drive
up some sparks.

9

'Strong and gentle, joy
takes all things forward.'

The breeze is lifting the edge
of the curtains where the window
is slightly ajar. I can hear it moving
already, stirring in the trees.

Well, a dip when the haze is not
yet off the surface of the lochan
could be the best time to begin.

'Practice makes perfect,
and use makes master.'

Though seduction on
a daily basis (real or
imagined) is not what
I wish to describe.

My shirt is on the bushes;
my towel is under a stone.

Just say the word
and I'll follow you in.

24 and 26 to Be Precise

Anthracene and pyrene
you wouldn't think to find
in nebular formations
or structures of that kind.

But in the Red Rectangle,
one thousand light years out,
their ultraviolet signatures
exist beyond a doubt.

So hydrocarbon molecules,
in long molecular chains,
came showering down in meteor-
ites or sundry cosmic rains.

Polycyclic aromatics
(like diesel engine fug)
are hydrocarbon ancestry
for bird and boar and bug.

Linked rings of carbon atoms,
organic matter base,
came early to the party
from turbulence in space.

The Welcome

She left the train at Polmont,
And walked away from me;
Her eye was dark, her face was fair,
Her mouth I could not see.

The day was cold, the light was thin,
The train was running late.
What welcome there in Polmont
Was waiting at the gate?

She crossed the bridge at Polmont,
Her step rang on the stair;
Her coat wrapped tight around her,
Pale ribbon in her hair.

I saw one stood beside the gate,
I saw her raise her glove.
No answering wave; no word came back,
The figure did not move.

The day was cold, the light was thin,
The train was running late.
What welcome there in Polmont
Was waiting at the gate?

Tod

A fox is before me, crossing the road
as I come down by the Mound. His body

is arched (a little bit arched) and he looks
at me sideways with care. His paws on

the cobblestones light and quick, his
narrow form clearly outlined, and I

loping down the grey flagstones
towards him. Neither one of us

pauses; though we skirt each other,
taking a short, canny look.

The moon, risen earlier, fat wee
clementine, is obscured now by cloud

or an angle of pediment. Tod slides
in by the gate of the National Galleries,

head low, ears pricked. My trail
is New Town and home; he, gaining

an entrance, carries his tail well up,
snout pointed just where he is headed.

Not, it turns out, for El Greco's testing
fàbula, with its monkey and candle,

a grinning man, the boy with pink
pursed lips – nor for any hint there

of vice or folly – but rather to the *Venus
and Cupid* of Lucas Cranach the Elder:

wisps of drapery, tendrils of russety-
blonde hair, and her gaze straight out

from the canvas. Tod fixed, ignores
the mischievous child with the golden

bow, his yellow, honey-coloured fox
eyes turned only to the lady: her small,

high breasts like persimmons, the line
of her back and belly; heavy red-gold

necklaces; neat feet, splayed toes.
Tod takes a slow turn or two closer,

edging in, you can sense it: her totem,
soon to be gone again, scarcely there

in the faintest smirr of Egyptian blue,
a shadow on the polished, parquet floor,

completing another low turn, claws, brush
tucked in, falls soft and sound asleep.

Everything

Everything is racing
   everything is vanishing

Everything is hosted
   everything is vanishing

Everything in the world that's seen
   everything is vanishing

All the angels rise and sing
   everything is vanishing

Everything that's clothed or bare
   everything is vanishing

Anything for a second there
   everything is vanishing

Everything is racing
   everything is vanishing

Everything is hosted
   everything is vanishing

Music, lovers, pillowslips
   everything is vanishing

Lightning, thunder, hail and rain
   everything is vanishing

In the mountains, on the streets
   everything is vanishing

Scissors, paper, rock, hands
   everything is vanishing

Everything is racing
   everything is vanishing

Everything is hosted
   everything is vanishing

The fox at night, the birds aloft
   everything is vanishing

Speedwell, crocus, lotus, rose
   everything is vanishing

With arms spread wide
   everything is vanishing

With soft foot-fall
   everything is vanishing

Everything is racing
   everything is vanishing

Everything is hosted
   everything is vanishing

Hear it now, see me now
    everything is racing
        everything is vanishing

Love each other, love each other
    everything is hosted
        everything is vanishing

4

Setting the Time Aside

'the sea is not salt enough'

1

Gently, gently gets
things going, as you
well know, and here's
the nub: the dust is up
afresh, and won't come
down till this is done.

Sydney, it's midnight
or shortly after, and I'm
trying to get you framed
in the shot: fixed plumb
in the cross-hair snap.

You're sat in a chair
before a desk, leaning
slightly towards me.
Window edge in;
brick wall behind.

You're puzzled or costive
ticked or cheesed off –
it's a bit hard to judge.
I'll have to take care
to get this straight:
not strain too long
nor squeeze a little tight.

Unlock the gate and let
us in. Unslip the leash
and let the beastie go.
Whatever you've got
to say to me, you'd
better say it now.
I'm all ears.

Would an upright man
betray his father?

Who broke the jade?

Who let the wild
buffalo down?

Surely to death we can offer
up some kind of an answer.

What are we meant
to be? What are we
meant to do? I'm
serious, now, Sydney,
we're starting to get through.

2

Five to the hour as
the long hand sweeps
round. What a puzzler
you've set out for
everybody. We've all
been tongue-tied
waiting for it too.

So where's the gap
or slap, or intersection,
which thresh-hold have
we set our toes to
transgress tonight?

(Hold on a bit, is
that the children starting
up? I think I hear
them through the wall.)

Sydney, Sydney, what
happened in the Pass of Glencoe?

Aye, to you I mean.
All that 'wiry, white-fiery
and whirlwind-swivelled snow.'

What did you mean
and what did it mean
tell me to come back?

3

Kenspeck, kenspeckle:
by means or dint of this
you may detect what
a rascal I actually am.

We ought to be able
to take enough out
now to bank the fire,
get paraffin and candles
in for the winter.

Never mind the fact
this looks like an office
in a business block
or some old language
cell waiting to be
demolished. Unclench.
Sing out. 'The tatties
are ower the side.'

What a laugh we used to have.

I'll give you a hand
if that's what you require.

You were never
one for writing 'too
much out of vanity' or
suppressing information
from neglect or disdain.

You always wanted
someone else to hear
it and tell it to.

Willie (chord change) I'm
singing as hard as I can.

I never heard the herrings
come home. I never sought
the sea in that way, no –
though I sought it right enough.

4

That's gone one:
it must be – and we've
still not come (though
it's moving on now) to
a song that wrecks the heart.

*I am a man upon
the land; I am a silkie
in the sea.* Nobody's
actually headed
that I can tell, without
any door provided.

Just you and that expression
of bricked-in pugnacity.

What leads to turbulence?

Who would you tap
to see if they're sound?

I envy you that
glacier calving: 'its
sudden momentary thunder.'

I saw one once
in Disko Bay
beneath the DC 7
stretch, mid-flight.

Full lunar eclipse
the self-same night.

5

Stirring, unstirring
the heavens complete
their happy slow rotation.

Ling and harebell: pinkest
pink and lightest fairest
blue on summer braes
shall still surround us.

6

Listen, that story about
the heilan shepherd does
not ring right to me.

And it's not that your words
are not yet come in to
their own true selves.
They have, or will do.

I *can* sing, by the way, I
said before – though
maybe not now.

I can dance.
(I swear to God).

Whatever you decide
to settle for, whatever
you take our mettle for,
whatever you use
that *kettle* for, we
like you nonetheless.

And there's bound to be
a way round somewhere.

Say the word 'dark'
often enough with clear
intensity. Ears and items
rapidly adjust. Cones
and eye-rods sharp adapt:
light quick quiver.

Fire and reset;
reset to fire again.

Who would you tap?

And who would you
shield from harm?

7

You can see the chop
on the water. Look over
the side and down.

Let's be nice to the pilot
though he seems to know fuck all.

Be nice. We're yawing
just a little bit.

At least no hydrocarbons
dumped on the tundra;

no frozen shit, nor
chicken dinners neither.

Elsewhere, things align.
Here's mebbe something to chew.
Shoo the crumbs off the table.

'The way is always there,'
says Kung Fu Tsu –
'it's the will that's wanting.'

Who gives a flying
fart (forgive me),
generous master? And, no
I don't think I can lend
you a couple of quid –
if that's what you are
leaning over to ask.

8

Bong–a-long, the clock
once more. Where were we?

The calving. Two
million tons of ice,
gravel, pockets of bacterial
decay: dropping like a
bomb in choppy water
deep down dark
in Disko Bay.

Always you knew
how to lower the tone
to a carrying whisper.

Saying, unsaying
the silence, the gentle
moon comes through
a break of cloud over
Clyde mouth and the Kyles
of Bute, stretching away to
Zennor and Gurnard Head.

9

Is that you there
yourself, caught on the hop
at the top of the Hope Street
stair? I see your face just
past the gas mantle,
taken up in some
grumpy divination.

Mantle glow or not
I'd recognize you.

That quiff, the growl
the gravel and shine once more.

I've got you now.
I might have known.

And look: the night's a pup.
The day will find us sound.
No flash (no need), no
word, no exit wound.

Having waited, having
wanted, here I am for
you now as sure as fate
as death as taxes all up
front and hot to trot.

10

Firing and unfiring
the shallows, a low sough
of wind from offshore
raises dust on the steps
as we go down: wading
in again to meet the salt
dark lance of the sea.

5

Tardigrade

Right at the outset I concede
the issue of size, substance; waive
it all, dismissed as an irrelevance.
It doesn't take much to squish or wish
me gone – a blip is all I am, for sure –
a twitch of next-to-nothingness:
four bits conjoined, eight legs, or six,
some pointy claws to clip or clasp,
pursue my most particular, undulant
way. The prying Goetz in his first
enthusiasm dubbed me 'water bear'
– *kleiner wasserbar* – a name I never
answer to, which nonetheless hints
at my gait, shape, my look-alike
in various vile – or even not so very
vilely – sentimental ways, as other
names may do: 'moss piglet', cutesy
and affected; tardigrade itself.

Who *says* I'm slow? After all, who
is primed to penetrate the depth
or full complexity of my arcane
dimensions? Who goes where I have
gone, who sees *one jot* of what it is
that I aspire to see or be or know?

Slow is a very scrappy, baseless,
futile, indeterminate term to match

or hint what I may get up to when
properly in the mood. As I abscond
and take my leave, if I go in my little
tun, abandoning likely surfaces;
if I can switch nolly-tankering away,
who's to follow? Who with any
sure conviction, firm or subtle
grasp, can say just what it is I do,
or how proceed, or how appear?

2

Well, speculation is a very fine thing.
Appearance too, but not enough to show
what's at the heart, and as for hearts,
I don't possess one. 'A barrel-shaped
body, with pairs of stubby, unjointed
legs.' The body, as I said, segmented.

The cuticle or chitin that wraps
me round I'll slough from time
to time, perhaps to lay my eggs in.
Look for me in mosses and lichens –
oh, yes, mis-appellation has a basis
in fact (dip some sphagnum in a glass
of water and there we are, as large as
life); but you might just as well have
opted for wall-baby, roof-worm,
beach-comber, dune-buggy: any insipid

link or tag to where I might reside,
since I am *anywhere*; or anywhere
a perch exists with water in the way.

3

As you might know, or can readily imagine,
waterless tissue cannot freeze. When I bump
along at three percent of bodily composition –
as opposed to eighty-five – not much can touch
me in that department. Desiccation, surely
a gladsome thing in itself, is also my starting
point to explain what otherwise sits strangely.

Ten years once I lay on a shelf, dried out almost
completely, before someone thought to rehydrate
and set me off again. Ten frigid days I've tumbled
in the vacuum of open space, absorbing ionizing
radiation and anything else that shoots this way
from our nearest stellar neighbour. High energy
UV and gamma rays in doses one thousand times
the strength that you would quickly find brings
down your blinds. I tagged along, a guest aboard
the *Endeavor* shuttle's final flight, (as you might
easily ascertain) and, after landing, when revived,
and prompted then to reproduce, I reproduced –
oh, yes, I did – and then I reproduced some more.

Now, here's a spur for invidious comparison:
I can take six times the pressure of the Mariana
Trench. Some complicated sugar, non-reducing,
protects my membranes. *More* than boil me,
more than freeze me – even briefly to one
degree above absolute zero – and I would still
be smiling upon return: if only I could smile!
Setting up home below solid ice, or swanning
around the dizzy summit of Annapurna barely
tests my tolerance, or tickles my capacity.

So, more to make it clear than rub it in: if
you were cryptobiotic quite like me, exactly
what would that amount to? Point zero one
percent of normal metabolic rate. Your usual
bumpetty-bumping lowered, in other words,
one thousand times. Next to nothing, as I said
before. Anhydrous, anoxic, osmotic, cryotic
conditions bounce off, as I, 'reversibly suspended',
entirely zonked away, sleep on (and on and on).

Going back, as we usually must, to basics:
nothing is assigned to breath or breathing.
The whole system swaps gas from out to in
and back again. Everything that matters
extends to *digestion*: stylets in the mouth
designed to pierce, the pharynx sucks, then
a little soup of cell mass and body fluids
(from spineless blips, both plant or algal)
takes a brief turn through the oesophagus,
passing then to the longer main track
and the usual points of exit.

I could go on – the 'brain', the ganglia,
the twin cam-shaft of the ventral chord
and its branching fibres. My 'rhabdomeric
pigment cups' (as eyes) – I sometimes use
them, sometimes not. I generally can sense
just where I am or what I'm up to (bristling
with intelligence of a kind) – enough
to move, to meet, to mate.

To make friends? – you might ask.
Well, not exactly. What decides how
many times I moult or excrete, just
how (or if) the two kinds – when there
are two kinds – interact and reproduce
is interesting, but accidental. What puts

what in where, what happens inside,
what transpires outside, how many
eggs are carried or attached, tucked
in the chitin (discarded or not), all that
matters of course – as apparatus,
mechanics, periphery – but *not much*.

It misses the point, the salient point;
and once again I don't have one: or not
that first, exquisite *plip* which marks true
palpitation. Even then, what and how
I am – or you – is still beyond the reach
of figures, prediction or taxonomy.

6

Points of resemblance, there
still must be, and some, without
quibbling, I will actually concede.
There are things too, of course,
which would not bear comparison,
and some of these, it's true,
I find quite hard to grasp.

What I like best about you,
if you'll permit me to say,
is your intermittent regard
or fondness for each other;

in addition to your more
recent curiosity about me.

It is an inordinate, shaky
business to be human, no
doubt; but, as an outsider,
affection seems to me a very
fine thing, and if (as I see it)
even briefly sustained, could
well comprise a true advantage.

Likewise – and I must confess
this took me quite aback since
I had not encountered it before –
awareness of life-lines outside one's
own is certainly commendable as
a means to perspective; even if
not allied to any real tolerance
or humility. Though that is not
beyond you. Nor love, that capital
distinction emerging between
us and what we choose to value.

Having said that, *value* (that's
the word; you tend to use it all
the time) has a consistency for me
that you would scarce appreciate,
nor even properly acknowledge.

Things slowly slip along the ecliptic:
familiar objects shift and drop. We wheel
and gyrate. But there's more to that than
angle of tilt, or the regular drift of celestial
co-ordinates. Cut the tremolo; hoist this
an octave. Look down and around as well
as up and over. Dust storms are especially
thick now over Yemen and the Gulf of Aden,
eventually thinning out over Suqutrá.
Pause first, then accelerate. Stop fussing
with numbers; taken too far it's flim-flam
and mummery. Make some adjustment,
get some perspective. On the Bering Sea
persistent northerlies have built up arches
of ice much larger than expected. While
a lingering ridge of high pressure fries roofs
in Duluth, bubbles tarmac in Scranton.
Milky green clouds of hydrogen sulphide
off the coast of Namibia kill fish aplenty,
but the birds rejoice that feed off their
carcasses. Look further out, and deeper in.
Don't talk the talk and miss your tip: slide
by the entrance just because it doesn't
whisper your name. Everywhere things
flow and on through, and it needn't
be me that comes to remind you.

8

It's a commonplace by now, I know, but no-one
can reconcile the very large with the very small.
Still, look at the case in point. No doubt, as I have
strained to establish, we share much more than
we miss. If we were to meld somehow: a touch
of you in me, me in you, what might we have
to answer for, or how might we conclude?
Consciousness counts; surely you can see that
beyond all your guesses, twinkling calculations.
If it's popped up once, it will certainly pop ten
million million times again. 'Things are not only
what they are' – 'Consciousness is intentional.'
Pin those ghostly markers firmly to the board
when all your world sinks down through ghastly
dross and bad behaviour. As for me, practising
the impossible, I recommend the same to you.
Extend. Alight. Extend some more, again.

9

Meanwhile, look there: that active
dark filament – that ribbon of gas
threaded over the solar disk. Another
surge, another eruptive prominence:
light bridges, faculae, plages, flares.
Whatever flows out on the solar wind
means to shape and destroy us. Oh,
to swim, though, in the polar plume
and the post flare loops! Wave fades
or phase shifts – it's hard to keep
track – but you surely must know
sunspot, corona, aurora. Bring everything to bear in the white flare light
and, believe me, large nothingness,
what's yours won't go by you.

Notes

Chopping Down the Beanstalk

'Fife' was the syllable randomly assigned for this contribution to Peter McCarey's *The Syllabary* – though the poem also strays into 'fie'. Robert Louis Stevenson provided the first quotation highlighted, and the second is from Charles Darwin's grandson, Bernard, who edited an early *Oxford Dictionary of Quotations* in idiosyncratic style. The alliterative line in the third stanza was Edwin Morgan's response to an image of armoured fish, discovered some way below the ancient kingdom.

True as Tides

See Donne's 'To His Mistress Going to Bed' and 'The Sunne Rising' – the rest of 'The Good-Morrow' too, why not?

Aye Plenty, an Mair

Glumsh or *Glunsh* are here just names, but associated with sour or grumpy looks. *Grizzel* is a good old Scottish name (from Grizelda). *Happit*: covered, wrapped (Fowk ging oot weel-happit agin the caal); *in aboord*: on board. *Golach* is short for horny-golach: an earwig or forky-tail. *Glit* is slime or mucous. *Drittle* (or druttle) is a general term of abuse – for someone who's too slow or a waste of time. *Fouter* (or *footer*) is likewise to dither, or somebody fussy and inept. A bit like *scutter*, which has the sense of faffing around in an irksome or unsatisfactory way. *Sotter* is another kind of tangled mess. *Fancies* are fancy cakes or biscuits. *Tablet* is Scots fudge, which is harder, but not less sweet, than other types. *Panjotteries* are pancakes. *Oofum-ploofums* are probably meringues. I only heard the word used once, vaguely indicating the more exotic or creamy items on a baker's crowded counter top. *Mindit* is remembered; *press* a cupboard or dresser, sometimes large and built-in. Galshach (pronounced *galshick*) where I grew up meant something tasty or attractive, but rubbish really, and likely a waste of money. *Redd* is to clear or tidy; *fleer* is floor. '*Bring aabody ben*' is take everyone through. The source and significance of the last two lines will no doubt vary with interpretation: especially the nature of the relatives, their origins and precise condition. Coincidentally, the poem was written just before the eruption of Eyjalfjallajökull in 2010.

Gavia Stellata

Starry speckles on the back of the red-throated diver give it its Latin name. The smallest of the loons – the *Gavidae* – it is variously connected to watery creation myths and to the heavens.

Camp Four

This poem came on the heels of a longer work, 'Setting the Time Aside', which was an attempt to engage with the inheritance and spirit – or shade – of W. S. Graham. 'Setting the Time Aside' works through various issues, drawing on some technical connections with Graham (like a three stress line) and making direct and indirect reference to his life and work. It shifts around in tone and circumstance, but it was meant to be directly personal: the voice or voices all came out of me addressing the other self one on one, and the engagement as well as any resolution takes place close to home.

'Camp Four', in contrast, sports and drifts in various dimensions, and the scattering of references to the remoter posts of theoretical physics and so on is part of a satirical displacement. The usual touchstones won't do, never last (the poet 'nothing affirmeth' says Sidney); but there is always something for poetry to make a noise about, provide a counter or reminder, sly or otherwise.

Wappenschaw

Wappen is a weapon: here waved present at a muster, or call to arms. *Schaw* is see or show; but could also be a little wood or copse or bosky grove.

Out of Magma, the Moon: a Witness

The weather on the slopes of Etna in Sicily in December is wintry enough. I was a guest of friends from Maniace. That small town in Catania is on the opposite side of the volcano from Taormina, where D.H. Lawrence wrote his poem 'Snake' in the high summer of 1923.

The small, semi-wild, black pig of the Nebrodi – *suino nero* – is especially delicious.

Hermeneutics

Muckle caa: much call or demand; *whins*: gorse; *wheeps*: whips; *speirt*: asked, requested; *baps*: buns.

The Daftie Names His Tunes

Apologies to anyone who takes offence at the title. Not in justification, but simply as an aside and in another context entirely, James Clerk Maxwell, the great Scottish theoretical physicist who formulated the laws of electromagnetism and reshaped our conception of the universe between Newton and Einstein and beyond, was given the nickname 'Daftie' at school, perhaps because of his home made clothes and rural accent.

The piece is taken freely from Villon's 'Ballade des menus propos', which begins: *Je congnois bien mouches en let.* Here *ken* (pronounced like *cane*) is know; *flees* are flies; *jaikit* is jacket; *quine* is girl or young woman; *aathin* is everything; *faa* is who; *yoakit* is yoked, active in work; *fit quidna* is what couldn't; *pit* is put.

Deil Tak the Hinmaist

This poem began its life in English as 'Unfinished Business' and was dedicated to 'CMG' – Christopher Murray Grieve, or Hugh MacDiarmid. A few years ago it decided it had another identity, pretty well transforming itself into (mostly North-east) Scots. The spelling usually is an aid to pronunciation. It should be read out loud, in the spirit of the old *flytings*: ritual insults freely exchanged. The chopped-out framework and various levels may appear Dantesque; but Dunbar and Rabelais are in the line-up too.

Hinmaist: hindmost; *ocht*: ought; *pilliwinkies*: finger or thumb screws, an instrument of torture; *girt yett*: great gate; *liggit*: lay; *skelpers*: strikers, whippers; *cuddies*: horses; *cleikit*: caught, hooked on to; *reikit*: stank; *tatties*: potatoes; *deedle-dabblers*: dilettantes; *dirlin*: reverberating; *Dodie*: George; *swickin and swyvin*: cheating and screwing; *daddy-lang-legs*: crane flies; *hoodie-craws*: hooded or carrion crows; *pooshin*: poison; *birslin*: bristling; *moo-fae*: mouthful; *couthy*: cosy, homely; *glisterin*: shiny; *sharn*: dung; *jow*: peal; *neist*: next; *syne*: then, subsequently; *kythit*: revealed; *tup*: ram; *draigelt yowes*: bedraggled ewes; *loons*: lads; *footerin*: hesitant, exasperating; *futtrets*: weasels or stoats; *hee-haw-hookum*: an indeterminate mischief; *hystet*: hoisted; *hizzies*: women-folk; *foosty*: fusty, mouldy; *fowk*: folk; *Finnan haddies*: a type of smoked haddock; *blaavers*: braggarts, boasters; *wecht*: weight; *blaw*: wind; *shouther*: shoulder; *sornars*: importunate scroungers; *sooks*: flatterers; *herriers*: robbers, plunderers; *haverers*: gabblers, people speaking nonsense; *gran chiels*: VIP's; *fantoosh*: extra fancy; *wifies*: women; *r.p.*: 'received pronunciation:' posh spoken; *parkins*: large round ginger and oatmeal biscuits; *merkin*: a pubic wig (some say) or the sine qua non; *seannachies*: wise men; story-tellers; *snoots*: snouts; *shooglers*: shakers; *trashtrie*: rubbish; *douce*: proper, respectable; *fushionless*: limp; vapid; *tail-toddle*: intercourse; *fussle*: whistle; *widdy*: wood; *thrapple*: throat; *mingers*: ugly wasters; *moochers*: cadgers; *flees*: flies; *wersh*: dull; *scoor*: scour, scrape; *duff*: pudding; *plooms*: plums; *slaw*: slow; *slaistert*: slathered; *faa*: who; *lest*: last.

Matter and Moisture

This poem emerged owing something to the *I Ching*, with much of the content boiled away; though it does save the central image of the Well.

24 and 26 to Be Precise

Derived from an article in *New Scientist*, March 20, 2004.

Setting the Time Aside

This piece got a start in 1999 and was finished ten years later. The photograph that figures at the beginning and later is a portrait of W.S. Graham (1918–1986), taken by Christopher Barker, and used as a cover by the *Edinburgh Review* in the eighties. Graham, born in 1 Hope Street, Greenock, at the mouth of the Clyde, lived much of his life down on the western tip of Cornwall. Although his poems and letters are a great and lasting achievement, even friends acknowledged the difficulties his personality occasionally created for himself and others. But the varied tone here is well within bounds of familiar Scottish practice: either deadpan or with a smile. The epigraph is part of Graham's response in receipt of poems sent by an acquaintance.

Tod

Tod is a Scots (and Northern) name for a fox.

Tardigrade

The creatures within the phylum *Tardigrada* were first discovered by Goetz in 1773. These microscopic invertebrates average out about the size of the full stop at the end of this sentence. They have the capacity (in their *tun*) to enter a state of reversible suspension: down to a death-like metabolic rate of 0.01%. This allows them to survive a range of extreme environments.